THE LANGUAGE
OF WOLVES

THE LANGUAGE OF WOLVES

Julio César Martínez Romero

Número de Control de la Biblioteca del Congreso de EE. UU.:	2015912282
ISBN:	Tapa Dura	978-1-5065-0728-6
	Tapa Blanda	978-1-5065-0727-9
	Libro Electrónico	978-1-5065-0726-2

Información de la imprenta disponible en la última página.

Fecha de revisión: 29/07/2015

Para realizar pedidos de este libro, contacte con:
Palibrio
1663 Liberty Drive, Suite 200
Bloomington, IN 47403
Gratis desde EE. UU. al 877.407.5847
Gratis desde México al 01.800.288.2243
Gratis desde España al 900.866.949
Desde otro país al +1.812.671.9757
Fax: 01.812.355.1576
ventas@palibrio.com
717402

CONTENTS

CHAPTER 1

The Eyes of the Beholder

I

Human beings are very selective with the information we pick up from the environment. We filter all the sensory input we receive and process it to build a comprehensible interpretation. We literally hear what we want to hear and see what we want to see. Among human beings, the more a personal reading of reality walks away from the actual experience, the more you would characterize such a perception as schizophrenic.

Each person who reads the few pages that constitute this manuscript will have read an entirely different book. Every reader will bring to this text his/her own academic background, personal history, beliefs and emotional needs. Imagine that a pack of orcas (killer whales, *Orcinus orca*) running away from a whaling vessel would proceed likewise, each of them reading reality in a subjective, personal manner, would that be adaptive? Indeed it seems that orcas do learn to recognize and avoid dangerous ships. Their personal histories change their perception and their response to the environment. Do orcas have minds? How do you know that other human beings have minds?

II

There is an enormous irrefutable amount of evidence that shows that some animals are highly intelligent, that they express deep and rich emotions and that they have developed sophisticated communication systems that allow them to coordinate group activities. Nevertheless, they probably do not possess symbolic languages defined in precise logical terms such as those that might not even exist among human beings. In this book I pretend to show that our notion of human languages has been idealized beyond any real human daily communication and any attempt to describe nonhuman communication with such definitions is entirely futile. I will also try to show that the subjective, manipulative, ambiguous and deceiving symbolic human languages are incompatible with the constant life threatening situations that animals face in their natural environments.

III

In order to build a dictionary of the language of another species, we would need to determine its function in the social interactions of the species.

If the information delivered has the purpose of changing the behavior of the receptor, then the response would be connected to the message. What information does the receptor need so that he can perform an expected task? What information does a college student need to solve homogeneous differential equations with constant coefficients? What information does a boy need to bake a strawberry cheesecake? What information do you need to read a text in Ukrainian? If you were given the right amount and type of information, your behavior would be modified by that information in a predictable way, would it not?

If the communication activity had the purpose of bonding with other individuals, then the content would be less important than the attitude. People sing, play baseball, tell jokes and dance to establish a cordial environment. The lyrics of the songs are meaningless to the desired result.

To grasp the meaning of a language we would need to know what its purpose is. How can we know the purpose if we do not understand what is said? We see two Albanian boys talking for half an hour, what is the purpose of their conversation? What are they saying? Without any additional clues, is it possible to understand the language of two human beings? Without any additional clues, is it possible to understand the language of two humpback whales?

IV

For centuries Egyptian hieroglyphs were considered decorative designs. In 1799, a French soldier, Pierre-François Bouchard, found a relic called the Rosetta Stone which consisted of three sections. The first one showed ancient Egyptian hieroglyphics; the second, demotic writing, and the third, a text in ancient Greek. Francois Champollion in 1822 discovered that some drawings were repeated in the segment with ancient Egyptian hieroglyphs following exactly the same pattern as the words present in the Greek section. It was thus that he realized that the stone contained the same text in the three languages. The Rosetta Stone was the basis for deciphering the hieroglyphs from ancient Egypt.

Modern dictionaries are the Rosetta stones that provide us with insight into foreign languages.

What are scientist looking for when they try to study the language of other species, such as dolphins? Are they looking for a Rosetta Stone, which will provide a good basis on which to build a dictionary that will enable humans to translate the sounds of other species into a human language?

V

Francine Patterson claims that Koko, a female lowland gorilla is able to understand more than 1,000 signs and approximately 2,000 words of spoken English. Irene Pepperberg reported that Alex, an African grey parrot, could speak more than 100 words and could classify objects and understand concepts. John Pilley trained Chaser, a female Border Collie, to retrieve one of more than 1000 different objects when listening to their individual names. These examples show us that some animals can build a mental Rosetta Stone in order to learn a part of our human dictionary. However, this does not mean that they have their own natural dictionaries to communicate with other individuals of their respective species.

VI

Let us walk into a bedroom with a young German mother belonging to a Protestant family, as she accompanies her daughter to bed and tells her a bedtime story. The girl's favorite is the story of how young King David fought and killed giant Goliath. For a person who only spoke Finnish it would be impossible to discover what the mother was telling her daughter in German. To be able to understand the meaning of the story, it would be useless to decode the actual environment of the mother and the girl, as the tale does not relate to it. How could a person from Finland witnessing this event learn the meaning of a human conversation? The truth is that people are isolated by language barriers even within our own species.

VII

Let us imagine that some extraterrestrial aliens want to study a group of boy scouts. The purpose of their research is to find out if human beings have an intelligent symbolic language. They use the most sophisticated audio recording and they register everything that humans do at the same time as they talk. The aliens follow the boy scouts on their way. The boys cross a stream, walk through the woods, drink water or stop at a mountain pass. With the most powerful computers and the most efficient algorithms they attempt to correlate human sounds with the specific circumstances happening at the time the sounds were produced. The alien hypothesis is that when the boys see a tree, they will say the word "tree" and with such data, aliens may develop a dictionary and discover a human grammar. Hikers begin their walk in silence. Later, they sing together. After a few minutes, some of them start telling jokes. Some jokes make everyone laugh while others produce an awkward silence, other jokes are interrupted by obscene remarks. The boy scouts stop to rest sitting on a fallen tree trunk and they talk about their girlfriends, and about every single promiscuous girl whom they have ever heard of. In the evening, they make a fire and tell terror stories before falling asleep.

When the aliens end their analysis, they conclude that the incessant chatter of human beings correlates neither with the environment, nor with the activities they are performing, thus it has no meaning. Their hypothesis assumes wrongly that we human beings say the words of what we see. It would be as if, when people are travelling in a subway train, when a lady with a baby gets in, all the passengers start repeating,

"Lady with child" or "old man", "handsome boy", or "thin woman".

VIII

Neither humans nor wolves go around our world reciting the words which describe what we see or what we do. Both among wolves and among boy scouts, vocal emissions reflect a collective mood and a general attitude, rather than providing a description of the environment. Among young boys vocal emissions may take the form of singing, telling jokes, horror stories or talking about girls. Like the songs of young people, the howling chorus of a pack of wolves is an activity involving the group that invites all to join cordially and with harmony.

IX

Another extraterrestrial alien is analyzing videos of Tchaikovsky's three ballets. Using the most powerful computers, the extraterrestrial is trying to discover from that huge amount of data, the key to human language. Its purpose is to find how the music and the story told in the ballet are correlated. He wants to develop a dictionary that translates sounds into actions. His search for a dictionary is in vain.

CHAPTER 2

From the Point of View of a Filmmaker

I

In 1997 I met a sixteen year old boy, Dragan Mladenovic, who lived in Murska Sobota, Slovenia. He spoke only Slovenian and I did not speak that language. He had studied algebra in high school. That was the language we both understood. He showed me a certain page of his Slovenian mathematics book. As soon as I saw the equations, I knew that it was the formula of De Moivre. I took a piece of paper and a pen and showed him without speaking how to solve the exercises. I solved one exercise first and then a second one. He watched silently. Then I wrote an exercise invented by me and handed the paper and pen to him. He looked at me in the eye and proceeded to do the same algebraic manipulations that I had done in the previous exercises. His answer was right. Then he continued to solve the consecutive exercises in his book having me as a witness to check his procedures. I did not understand the instructions of the exercises in Slovenian. We shared a universal symbolic language, algebra, and that was enough for me to achieve the purpose of teaching him how to solve two dozen increasingly difficult exercises.

II

If you play the piano very well, it does not matter in what country you are, or what language people surrounding you speak, if you have a piano and a piano score, you will be able to play. Ballet and concerts are performed all around the world and there is not a language barrier to understand them. If people have been trained to listen to such music and to watch such spectacles, the language of the country will not be a hindrance to grasping the meaning of the sound symbols.

Music scores and algebra are sets of symbols which mean something only to those who have studied them. In a certain way Koko, the gorilla, also learned a symbolic language that allowed her to understand human signs. Her learning process was not essentially different to a person learning algebra. Neither sign language nor algebra are natural languages for gorillas or humans, respectively. However, once learned, those symbolic languages provide a window to access a world of communication with others who know the same signs.

III

How do you recognize a dog, when you see one? There are dogs of all sizes, colors, tempers, and shapes. How do you know that each one of them is a dog? Plato explained that besides the individual dogs that exist in the world, there is a concept of the dog. That concept is formed in a person's mind. It includes all dogs that have lived, are living, will live in the future, and even animated 2D or 3D, sculpted, described in literature, and painted dogs that have never existed. The words that human beings use in their everyday conversations represent those concepts. When a mother tells her children, "it is cold, put on your coats", the children understand the meaning of the concepts, "cold" and "coat". Humans have a very large collection of concepts, thousands of them, and use words to express them.

When a parrot, a pig or a dog is asked to fetch a plastic ball, the animal will bring one, it does not matter what size or color the plastic ball is. If it is asked to search for a small plastic ball, then the animal will narrow its definition and bring the required object that represents the concept. These animals have developed the concept of plastic ball in their minds and they recognize any object that corresponds to it. They have been taught to associate such concept to the human voice pronouncing a word. This does not mean that in a natural environment the animals would have sound symbols for the different objects grouped in concepts.

IV

Certainly an African wild dog distinguishes individuals that belong to its pack and those strangers to it. A wild dog knows what zebras, wildebeest, impalas, lions, hyenas and human beings are. When they are hunting, they recognize weak, diseased or crippled animals and choose them as preys.

In an effort to reintroduce African wild dogs to the former ranges from where they had been exterminated, a pack was released in a reservation. The dogs did not know, because they had not learned such a skill, how to choose the easiest prey to catch. Each dog chased a different healthy animal and they were never able to make a single kill. They weakened and finally they all starved to death. This means that the ability to choose preys has to be learned. This ability represents a classification and the development of concepts. The vital classification of weak, crippled, diseased, old, or slow means the difference between life or death for a wild dog. It cannot be inferred that African wild dogs have special sounds to reflect the concept of adequate prey. If instead of African wild dogs, we were talking about Border Collie dogs, these concepts could be associated to the words of their trainer. The association in dogs of concepts and sounds is an artifact introduced by the human need to control the behavior of the dog. It does not reflect a natural activity of canids in the wild. African wild dogs have the concept of crippled herbivore, and they classify the zebras they see according to the concept. Then they choose the right zebra to chase. They have concepts, but that does not mean that they have words for the concepts.

V

Pasolini, an Italian filmmaker, theorized that a movie is a sequence of images, which he called im-signs. Watching a movie is grasping the meaning of a succession of images and sounds. He claimed that films are made of the same material as dreams and memories. He wrote that whenever you remember something, a sequence of images is awoken, attached to that memory. For example, you are watching a film and you see an actress there. "Who is she?" you wonder. "Where have I seen her?" In seconds your mind searches among hundreds of probable images and then the memory of a TV series prevails. Once again, hundreds of images from that series gather, until you remember, "Oh, yes! She is the young queen in that series!"

Pasolini proposes that there are two different types of languages, spoken/written languages (len-sign languages) and oniric languages (im-sign languages such as movies, dreams, and memories). The two types are separated by fundamental differences. Len-sign languages express reality with a dictionary of symbols, whereas im-sign languages express reality through images of reality itself.

Im-sign languages symbols cannot be gathered in a dictionary, because they are infinite in their nature. Each im-sign captures a unique unrepeatable moment of reality. Len-sign languages have a grammar, im-signs can combine almost chaotically, stylistically not grammatically.

To better show the difference between len-sign and im-sign languages, Pasolini explains how a writer works. From the dictionary of the language used by his social group, a writer choses a set of words and as he wishes, he places them within the margins of grammatical and historical usage. A filmmaker searches for im-signs in his imagination. There is not a finite set of socially recognized fixed images and there are no grammatical rules to use images. However, this does not mean that the filmmaker invents the im-signs from scratch. Almost everyone in his subculture will recognize the im-sign. For example, im-signs for a wolf, a dolphin, or a fawn are in everyone's mind, but not the exact precise wolf that the filmmaker will include in his movie.

In len-signs, abstract words, such as intelligence, evoke abstract concepts. Abstract concepts do not exist in im-sign languages. Im-sign languages are constituted by images, and images are concrete, objective, never abstract. Therefore, Pasolini concludes that it is not possible to express philosophical reflections in im-sign languages.

We are so anthropocentric in our scientific research that we claim that animal languages must be similar to human languages, in order to deserve such a denomination. We search for evidence of len-sign languages in animal interactions. How can we be certain that im-sign representations do not exist in the animal world? Would im-sign mental representations qualify as a language?

CHAPTER 3

Nonhumans Communicate

I

How do we understand a film? Because we learn how to. Many people cannot undrestand a movie with an alternate structure, surprising twists, complex characters and revealing turning points. They simply get lost. They were not trained to "read" multidimensional narrative. They are used to watching clear linear stories with prototypical protagonists and antagonists. Are animal minds capable of grasping the meaning of a sequence of im-signs as a representation of reality? When do such sequences become too complex for them to understand?

II

The architecture of a dolphin's brain is different from the human's. Its auditory center and its visual center are next to each other. Some researchers speculate that the information received back from an echo is processed by the dolphin's brain to build an image associated to that echo. If this were true, when a dolphin hears the echoes generated by another dolphin, they would probably be translated into images. That would mean that all dolphins would be simultaneously sending sounds, and all would be receiving everybody's echoes/images back. Instead of having a conversation, all dolphins would be simultaneously and constantly posting echoes/images on their "Facebook pages", the acoustic environment of the dolphin school. When a dolphin publishes something interesting, it catches everyone's attention.

Among humans, the sequence of photographs posted on the timeline of a person's Facebook wall is more complicated that the most vanguard underground, hipster film. It has neither dramatic structure nor grammar. Its sequence does not have a narrative purpose. Any storytelling derived from it would be an interpretation artifact. If after being published on the walls, the posts disappeared, any artificially imposed plot would fade away. The meaning retrieved from the posts, would be a meaning attributed to them. Pieces of personal life experiences would be exposed for a moment for anyone to see and then they would vanish in the vastness of the ocean of a social network. The posting of photographs in a Facebook wall is not a first person narrative. If such were the communication environment of dolphins, it would not make any sense to try to decipher their conversations, because there would be none.

III

On January 9, 2013, I dreamed that a young man had huge claws that allowed him to climb walls. He was a werewolf who wanted to protect a young lady who was trapped in the werewolf castle. The lady had been turned into a black and white heifer. She was a werecow. Being a heifer, she was in constant danger among wolves. Another young werewolf wanted to help the first one to rescue the heifer. I myself, threw large chunks of raw meat to entice the other wolves in the castle to move into the inner yard and distract them to allow the young werewolves to take the heifer away. After escaping, one of the young werewolves was missing. The heifer was very sad because one of the werewolves was not with us anymore.

Please indulge me, and let us suppose that the auditory and visual centers are close to each other in my brain cortex and the visual information of the dream I have just recalled is automatically translated into a sequence of sounds, which I will call the "dream song". I sing my "dream song" out loud and another being of my same species listens to it. Its visual and auditory centers are also close together and the song is translated back into the images of my dream. I sing my dream and whoever listens to my song, sees the images. Would that not be something amazing? Well, this does not happen, neither among humans, nor among dolphins, humpback whales or wolves.

I live among wolves and all the time they are either sleeping, eating, hunting the occasional unlucky squirrel, or playing. They are never chatting. The howling choruses have the purpose of determining the location of each pack member. The choruses last for a minute and a half and besides being terribly noisy, they do not have any poetic information. The life of my wolves is a very monotonous routine, nothing happens worth telling the others. If they dream, their dreams must be very similar to each others' too. I do not believe a wolf would get any valuable information from a colleague's dream recollection. It would not teach the other wolf anything worth learning.

IV

Nonhuman vocalizations clearly have a purpose. If you make a catalog of dog vocalizations and another catalog of sperm whale clicks and creaks, you will find that in each case certain sounds and frequency of sounds are associated to specific circumstances. A dog has a specific bark when it wants to go out for a walk and it has another very different threatening territorial bark. Nevertheless, the special bark the dog uses as an invitation to play, serves a definitive purpose and it is probably not a conversation opener, except if you would consider a chasing game an acted conversation with the purpose of strengthening the bonds in a group. Communication is not an algorithm procedure to transmit precise information. It has the purpose of reinforcing the emotional bonding among the members of the group.

V

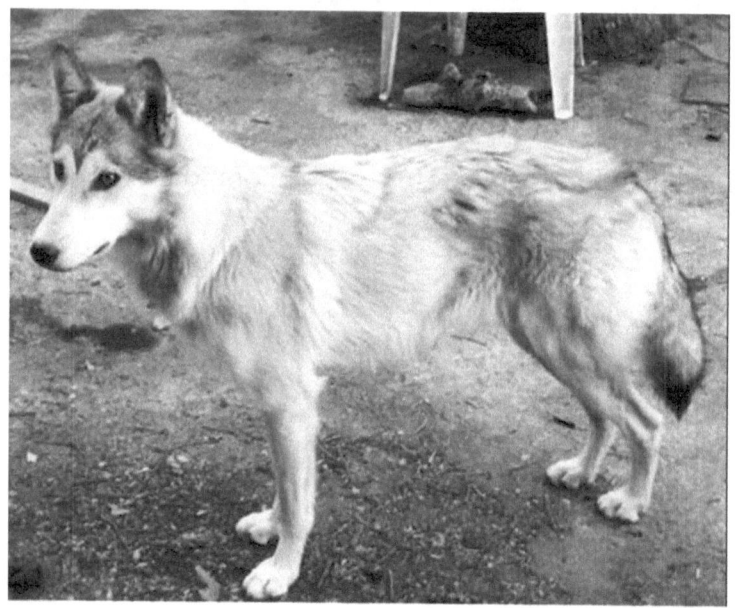

Wolves communicate primarily through sight, sound and smell. The code signal is not subject to personal interpretation. If a female wolf in heat urinates close to another female, that act, together with the exact position of her ears, her lips, her mane, tail, legs, posture, and her vocalizations conveys a precise message. A dictionary of hundreds of combinations exists for a wolf. Each combination has a unique meaning. Once he has received a precise message from another wolf, the receiver responds with another exact combination of auditory, physical and olfactory cues. In this way, the two wolves communicate clearly. For example, one wolf tells another: "I am superior to you and I'm in a bad mood". The other replies: "Please let's play." The first wolf changes his body language and vocalizations and replies: "I'm not in the mood". His correspondent also changes its message and says: "Hey, I look like a helpless puppy." Thus a talk between wolves operates. The set of body language, odor and sound signals constitutes a precise and error-free performance catalogue.

VI

Two elderly men, one with conservative ideas, and the other with socialist ideas are having an argument. The socialist has a stomachache and is in no mood to engage in the discussion. He says goodbye and walks away, but the other old man follows him, shouting, "all Socialists are thieves." He yells the same phrase over and over again, while the other is walking away. The scene looks exactly as when a small dog is barking at another dog walking away.

VII

For ten years I lived in an aviary with a dozen Red-lored amazons (*Amazona autumnalis*). I spent more than three waking hours among them every day. They slept around me. When they were ten years old, they reached sexual maturity, and a pair of them became very territorial. They attacked me and the other birds viciously and killed four of the other birds in my absence, they literally tore them to pieces. The aviary was not large enough for them and I had to give my parrot friends away.

I learned some things from this tragic experience. There were two behaviors that were difficult to ignore. One of them consisted in one parrot hanging from a leg upside down from a high place, screaming and flapping its wings very quickly. I looked up in books and in the internet for an explanation for this behavior. The consensus was that the bird was trying to call its owner's attention by pretending that one of its legs had got caught and that it needed to be freed. My interpretation is very different. Once a bird started this behavior, the others would follow. Their pupils dilated and contracted during their frantic display. The shiny red patches that form the "specula" on their spread wings were fanned at a high speed. They were evidently excited. I am sure that this was an aggressive territorial display, a warning. I do not think that they were addressing each other with this message. I think that their display was directed at me. It may seem paranoid but I consider that this was a menacing behavior. I was in the center of a circle, surrounded by a cylinder of green screaming birds at the level of my head, bombarded by almost constant iridescent bright red flashes. If I had been a minor threat in the jungle, a monkey or a coati, this collective warning would have persuaded me to leave as soon as possible.

VIII

There was another behavior that called my attention. Parrots are seldom quiet. They seem to be chatting all the time. Were they having a real conversation? Were they exchanging ideas and talking about their personal experiences? What was the purpose of such a perpetual prattle? I have an explanation to this behavior. When a sudden strong noise, a strong earthquake, a helicopter or some other hazard frightened them, all the birds were motionless and quiet. Some of them moved noiselessly to some place where they could hide and all the time, they would be completely silent. On the other hand, on the event of a sudden movement of mine or a dog's, or if I dropped something and made some noise, then the birds would send a loud shrieking alarm call. In other words, a threat is made public with an alarm call.

Complete silence means serious danger. In contrast, constant chatter is a mutter to reassure everyone that everything is right. If you are facing an implacable predator, how do you warn the others without turning the predator's attention to you? Silence is the ultimate proclamation of peril.

The absence of silence is the comforting perpetual chirping of parrots.

IX

A basketball game is a very fast moving coordinated activity. If you watch a final game of the NBA or of the Olympic games, you will realize that each player is attentive to every other player in his visual field, friend or foe. In the midst of the action, there is little vocal communication in terms of discussing strategy. This highly sophisticated team work is not encoded in the human genes but it has to be learned, mostly by imitation.

If you have witnessed how a wolf pack hunts in a high grass prairie with little visibility, you will realize that wolves do a lot of listening. They are constantly looking for any sign of movement either from their fellow hunters or from the prey and they try to keep the pace as fast as they can, directing their movements towards the center of activity.

Coordination, neither in the middle of a basketball game nor when a wolf pack is hunting, results from vocal (len-sign) instructions. Decisions are made the very moment the outcome of the situation changes. Wolves hunting in high vegetation trust their ears to locate where the other players are. Killer whales and dusky dolphins cooperatively herd anchovies or herrings into tight spheres to hunt them more easily. Very probably the clicks that the cetaceans emit have either the purpose of intimidating their preys or to let other whales know what their position is in an environment with reduced visibility. Listening to clicks would be like paying attention to the rustle of the bushes and such auditory clues let each wolf know where other pack members are. It would be very unlikely to assume that basketball players, wolves and cetaceans are holding a conversation of any kind under such circumstances.

CHAPTER 4

To Isolate a Group

I

What non-genetic information do individuals need to share in order for the group to survive and perpetuate their genetic information into the future? How do human societies benefit from a narrative of imaginative fantastic happenings? What is the advantage for a human group over another to tell vampire and werewolf stories as their group lore?

A human language in which the group's mythical religion is told, isolates the group from other individuals who speak different languages and hold different beliefs. Language and stories told in a certain language glue a human group together and hinder the interaction with other groups. Thus, the genetic pool of the group remains untainted from the genetic variations that can be introduced from other groups.

A boy in Argentina learns to speak Spanish and to play soccer, a girl in Saint Petersburg learns to speak Russian and to dance ballet. Young orcas in the Peninsula de Valdez learn to strand on the sandy beach to be able to catch baby sea lions, whereas orcas in the Johnston Strait learn to chase salmon, and transient orcas entering the Gulf of California learn to chase and hunt large whales. Lions learn to hunt elephants, wildebeest or kudus, depending on the abundance of prey herbivores in their territories. Sperm whales also have cultures, a set of behavioral traits learnt in their groups, which allows them to recognize other members of the group and that are adaptive to their local circumstances.

II

Orcas (*Orcinus orca*), which some people call killer whales, have two contrasting ways of living. Some are resident, eat mostly fish and have a large repertoire of vocalizations. Others are nomadic, transient in their visits to some region, and they are mainly hunters. Transient orcas eat seals, dolphins and hunt large whales. Because it is a disadvantage for them that their preys discover their presence, they are quieter and their vocalizations are less varied.

It has been reported that the catalogs of vocalizations differ for orcas belonging to different pods. These different sets of calls are called dialects. Resident orcas from different geographical regions use different dialects. Transient orcas' dialects are more distant from the residents' than the different residents' among themselves. Transient and resident orcas tend to avoid each other. When captive orcas coming from different regions use different dialects, after some time they learn the dialect the other orcas use. In the wild, orcas keep within the boundaries of their group, sharing the same dialect but it seems that they mate outside of their dialect group, thus reducing the risk of consanguinity.

CHAPTER 5

The Perfection of Human Language

I

Stephen and Arthur agree to meet for lunch at 1:00 in a certain cafeteria at their university. They both know that Stephen has a very busy schedule that day and that he will have to drive for at least 45 minutes in heavy traffic to get to the university. On the other hand they both know that Arthur will have a free morning and it will take him ten minutes tops to walk from his residence to the cafeteria. Stephen hurries a lot and walks into the cafeteria at 1:00 sharp as agreed. Arthur arrives at 1:50. His argument is that he arrived late on purpose. Arthur knew that Stephen would be very busy that day and he assumed that Stephen would not arrive on time and would feel guilty to be late. So Arthur inferred that because Stephen would surely arrive late, it would be a relief for him to realize that Arthur had arrived late too. Stephen complains, "It was a mutual agreement that we would be here at 1:00. I strained to get here on time in spite of the very busy day I had". Arthur replies, "that does not mean anything. Even though I had a free day today and I could have easily arrived on time, I knew that you would be at least 45 minutes late. Thus, I chose to arrive late" If you think that such a train of thoughts is far fetched, you should watch and listen to people more closely. Most arguments of people make no logic sense at all. We have idealized human len-sign communication as if it were coherent. Somehow we extrapolate that idealization and expect to find a logical structure, inexistent among humans, in nonhuman communication systems.

II

I interviewed dozens of people. Before asking them a question, I described to them a certain behavior among human beings and asked them if they had witnessed anything like that any time in their lives. Every single person told me at least a couple of recent instances of such behavior. My interview consisted in asking each person if it had happened to her/him that another person had asked her/him for a personal favor. For example, I would tell the interviewed, Peter asks you, "please let me stay in your place for a couple of days." Later on Peter is certain that he is the one doing you the favor. Peter says, "you should thank me for staying at your place, because all that food in the fridge would have rotten if I had not consumed it." Everyone I interviewed could give me lots of examples of people who, instead of being grateful because you did something for them, they expected you to be grateful to them. With these examples I am trying to show that we idealize human thoughts and their len-sign expression as if human languages expressed logical inferences and clear arguments. People's thoughts are not logical, the communication of their ideas is not logical either.

III

Another function of the use of the word among humans is to convince someone else to do something that is not part of his or her expected responsibilities. For example, a girl really likes cats and her boyfriend does not stand them. She convinces him to adopt a cat. As time goes by, the cat's care becomes the boy's full responsibility. Every other day, he has to change the cat's litter box. Every day he gives it milk and pellets. The boyfriend thinks, "How nice! I love her so much, but I hate cats. How is it possible that I even have to clean the sand box of the cat?" He thinks, "If she really wants a cat, why doesn't she take care of it? The smell of the litter box is unbearable and I have to be doing all these tasks that I hate." Many people see a relationship like a sports competition, a contest of wills. They are right, every time a person persuades a second person to do something that he does not want to do, the first person rewards his need to be in control at the expense of the relationship. If you win control, you lose the person. Language is a powerful means to manipulate someone to do what you want him/her to do. Language is a tool to control other people.

IV

Humans have lost the ability to read body messages and we pay attention only to the meaning of words. For example, a boyfriend, through his body posture, eye movement and inflections of his voice is telling his girlfriend, "I am an irresistible young man and you are a naive fool girl easy to seduce".

However, with his spoken words he asks, "How is it possible for me to have these feelings for you? I did not know I was capable of so much love. I had never felt like this before. You are different from any other girl and you make me feel special. I never thought I could love someone as much as I love you". His body language changes and now he means, "Surely you will start your boring babbling and I will interrupt you by kissing you on the mouth." The girl lacks any ability to interpret body language because she wants to believe that his words are true. She needs to feel loved and accepted and she is desperate to find someone who will consider her a unique and irreplaceable human being. She feels that her parents are too busy taking care of their own problems and concerns and meeting their own needs. Her parents do not provide the environment of affection that she requires, whereas this enchanted prince fulfills her need to love and to be loved.

CHAPTER 6

Life is Indeed a Novel

I

There is a continuum in human communication that goes from a mood establishing nonsensical chit-chat that enforces the bonds of a social group, to the highly complex technical protocols that are needed to perform neurological surgery, build a DNA sequencer, send a probe to outer space, elaborate tactic war decisions or implement social programs in another country. It is obvious that non-human animals do not have the ability to develop technology or perform coordinated tasks that require the accumulation of information over generations.

II

In their book, The Seven Shades of Guilt, Sergio I. Carrera and Julio Cesar Martinez Romero wrote, "Its hind insect legs made a sound like hooves hitting the metal floor of the hall. Its head, which was like a wasp's, had a transparent exoskeleton through which its big brain could be seen. On the brain, complex trajectories of bright blue light showed. Suddenly, the light of its brain changed color and became a red glare. The creature paused, listening, still staring at the corner where the hall ended and where it should have to turn. Everything was silent." These words describe something that does not exist in our life experience. They are understandable for a person who speaks English and when the words are read, they evoke images of the nonexistent. For a person who speaks only Russian, these words are meaningless. If you do not know the Japanese language and see a text in that language, there is no way to understand its meaning. Stories are universally told, however they are understood only for those who share the same language.

III

Story telling is one of the most time consuming activities that depend on the use of language among human beings. We dream at night, wake up and read the newspaper, watch the news on TV or listen to news when traveling to our jobs. We talk to people, they tell us their news or gossip, we read, write, ponder, plan or evaluate narratives on whatever subject interests us. When we are by ourselves, we daydream, remember, or fear stories in our minds. When we have free time, we listen to songs, watch movies, go the theater, watch TV series, go out with our friends and we listen or express our worries or plans in the form of a narrative. Such a pervasive function of language makes us wonder if it surged abruptly in human beings or started developing earlier in a simpler way among other animals. If we knew more about the neurological correlates of storytelling, we would be able to detect its patterns of brain activity in other species, under the hypothesis that our brain structure and function is similar to that of other animals. This hypothesis is highly improbable in dolphins, whose brains have diverged considerably from ours in the last 50 million years.

Children and older adults are prone to repeating the same stories with exactly the same wording, songs have the same requirement, as do theater plays. How ancient is this recitative story telling? Is it what really distinguishes us from other animals or do their minds have similar functions?

IV

When we have just woken up from a dream, for the few seconds before it fades away, images and feelings linger in our minds and make us unrest. Sometimes we deliberately try to remember the dream, to tell it as a story to ourselves.

Besides dreaming, our human mind also performs activities such as daydreaming, planning and remembering. In all those activities there is an evident narrative of a sequence of events.

V

Ismael is dreaming. He dreams that his late mentor and friend Julio García is having dinner with Ismael and his mother. When Julio García was alive, they held similar dinners dozens of times. In his dream, Ismael ponders, "how is it possible for the mind to so clearly recreate in a dream, images, attitudes and the voice of a deceased person?"

A female cat lived with an old lady for many years, the cat's whole life. The lady died and the cat was taken to another house with strange people. Thousands of times, she shared the old lady's bed. Is it not possible that the cat remembers the lady she loved? Might the cat miss her beloved companion? Could it be that the cat sometimes dreams that she is on the same bed as her late dear owner? The main difference is that Ismael is able to share his dream through a len-sign narrative, while the cat's dream is her own.

VI

A white tail doe once barely escaped from a human hunter. She remembers that human beings are threatening. Each time she detects the presence of humans, she displays all her alarm signals so that her family might be safe. Her family profits from her experience but she is not able to tell them what happened to her, she cannot explain why men are dangerous. There is not a story associated to her behavior.

VII

We humans are storytellers. Our languages evolved to be efficient for narration. We shaped our languages so that they would be able to describe our memories, our fantasies, our dreams and fears. Our languages reflect inner experiences, not the outer world. Nevertheless, for the person to be functional and sane, inner perception should be similar to the outer reality. However, words are used to express deliberate lies, wishful fantasies, proposed plans, all of them far away from reality.

VIII

We interact with other people and we tell our thoughts, we comment on current events or discuss work, study or exchange business related information. Would apes, elephants, parrots, wolves or dolphins engage in such behavior? Evolutionary speaking, why would this conduct be adaptive in human beings and not in other animals? What makes human stories worth telling? Probably, the answer to this question is that through our storytelling we teach others our experiences.

IX

When a grizzly bear eating the carcass of an elk, growls at an approaching pack of wolves, the growl is a warning to prevent them from getting closer. The growl is not intended to teach the wolves but to keep them away.

Certainly, distress calls, wolf howling, other animal vocalizations and body language, encode messages in order to modify the behavior of the receiver. In a certain way, they are instructions. The response promoted by them does not surge from imitation. Growling sends a message to other animals, either of the same social group or even of different species. However, none of such behaviors could be considered teaching.

There is a breakpoint in teaching when instead of imitating, an instruction is received and followed. A larger brain means an increased capacity to learn. Is that knowledge acquired only through observation and personal experience or can it be transmitted through a narrative of instructions? Up to some level of complexity, elephants, dolphins, some dog breeds, apes and parrots perform activities they are not watching and imitating, but derived from a human instruction. Is this behavior of nonhuman animals prompted by human needs or would they act so spontaneously? For example, border collies can learn to perform certain acts rewarded by their human trainers, but their cubs will learn only from their mother's example, that is from imitation, not from their mothers' instructions.

A lady can teach a little boy and a border collie to follow the instruction, "go to the shelf and fetch the cloth ball", and both of them will bring her the correct object. However, a border collie will not teach its cubs to obey that instruction. In contrast, the boy can be asked to explain to another child to follow the same instruction, and he will.

X

We would expect function to shape the structure of language. If animals do not teach each other, why should we expect their languages to share a structure similar to ours?

When an adult lion, eating a zebra that the pride has just hunted, growls to a teenage cub that slowly crawls to the zebra, the message is to keep away. The growl will be the same if it is a hyena or another member of the pride. The message is to keep away, not to teach the receptor of the message. The teenage lion will learn from the experience, nonetheless.

XI

In a certain way, even highly sophisticated behaviors among humans, are learnt by imitation. If a teacher explains and shows on the blackboard how to solve differential equations with Laplace Transforms, and his students learn by repeating the strategy in a similar problem, there is an imitation of the behavior involved. Learning how to play a ballade of Chopin for piano from a music score is to try to imitate a music performance from a set of instructions written in a code. Reading the instructions to install a hardware component in an electronic device is to try to imitate a sequence of actions proposed by a manual. In all these instances, there is an intention to teach and a will to learn. When a mother killer whale teaches her cub how to strand on a beach to catch a young seal or sea lion, the mother expects the young whale to learn and the cub strains to acquire the ability. That teaching experience involves an imitation process.

XII

We are a teaching species. We are obsessed with sharing information. Our languages are shaped to be efficient in storytelling and therefore, teaching. Furthermore, there is another use for story telling in a human society, expressing guilt.

XIII

Sometimes, and in spite of having acted with the best intentions, everything turns out wrong and we feel guilty. Our remorse lies in comparing two presents: the actual moment resulting from our misstep, and a hypothetical one, in which everything should be better because there we did not blunder. The blame is the longing for a nonexistent better future. Guilt is the pain of having destroyed an ideal future. With guilt, we regret our contribution to the imperfection of the universe. We would have liked like our contribution to be perfect, but perfection does not exist.

We forget that, having acted in good faith, we tried to make the best decision, but ignorant of the consequences, we were wrong. We blame ourselves for not having predicted the future accurately. We make mistakes because we do not know the consequences of our actions due to the uncertainty of the future. We move blindly on the timeline, not knowing what monsters or wonderful surprises lie ahead. However, each of our actions is only one of the many factors that determine the future. In order to express and understand our guilt, we imagine and regret what could have happened. We tell ourselves the story of the perfect future where we did not make mistakes. Feeling guilty and telling ourselves the story of the two futures, the one damaged by our mistake and the other wonderful one is a way of teaching ourselves not to make the same mistake again. Guilt is a punishment that has the purpose of teaching ourselves to avoid errors.

XIV

Why would narrative be present among human beings as the key element of teaching and why would it not be important among nonhuman social animals?

Some functions need to be performed in order for the group to survive and some individuals are better suited to fulfill those tasks. Some lionesses are better huntress, others are better watchers, others are better mothers and nurses, some are more aggressive when facing danger or confronting trespassing lions. More than individual biographies, role descriptions would better explain the dynamics of a group.

On the other hand, each human person has a deep fear of his/her own death, perceived as the end of his/her individual life. Human beings need to be considered irreplaceable. A healthy fear of death is needed for all animals to survive. However, a good huntress can be substituted by another better huntress. Among human beings death is equivalent to being forgotten and the only way to defeat death is by transcending, by being remembered as individuals.

The biography of an individual is worth remembering if the human being described is different. The only way to be unique is to be original. There is a certain cult for difference, uniqueness and individuality among human beings. A biography is a narrative with the purpose of preserving the memory of a person that has been remarkable for his group. A language, adequate for narrative, responds to the need of preserving the memory of individuals. Very probably among nonhuman animals there is no need to have a narrative language because there is no cult for personality in their groups.

We human beings are in a constant search for someone to listen to our personal news, to our gossip and our ideas. We appreciate a good listener and are bored with people who monopolize conversations with their narcissistic infatuations. We plead for other people to recognize our uniqueness. We detest when other people do not even bother to learn our names. We are hungry to teach others the value of our personal experiences. We expect that whatever we say will be worth learning for others.

Why else would I have spent so much effort writing this book? If nonhuman animals do not have these narcissistic needs, why should they have a language to remember the life stories of certain individuals?

CHAPTER 7

The Story Inside a Story

I

Have you ever seen a couple of kids playing with their toys, small dinosaurs, little cars, dolls, or whatever figures they have to play with? The essence of the game is an implicit "let's pretend" narrative. In a certain way when you see two wolves chasing a third one, it is also a representation. Two wolves pretend that they are hunters and the third pretends that it is their prey. Thus, the game is an acted symbolic narrative. But, is it a conversation? Is it a language expression?

II

Ivette, a young woman is Daria's mother. When Daria was four years old, Ivette married and had a second daughter, Natasha. Ivette was devoted to Natasha. She justified this disproportionate attention explaining that younger children require more care than older ones. The truth was that for Ivette, Natasha represented the dream of having a family; that is, a husband and children. It was evident for all, especially for Daria, but not for Ivette that there was a great difference in the way the mother treated her two daughters. In spite of being a very intelligent girl, Daria used to upset her mom repeatedly committing the mistakes that most bothered Ivette. For example, Ivette found it unbearable that Daria opened her bag, took out Ivette's money and left their house without asking for permission to buy candy, often taking Natasha with her. How could Daria be so smart and at the same time not be able to understand how much her mother resented such behavior and repeatedly offended her in such a way? This fixed pattern of behavior represents a dialogue between Yvette and Daria and could be transcribed as follows:

Yvette: I'm busy with Natasha and I cannot assist you now, Daria.

Daria: I will bother you so much that you will have to pay attention to me.

Yvette: You did something that I find unbearable and now I have to distract myself from Natasha to scold you.

Daria: That is what I wanted. You would not listen to me. Finally, I achieved my goal. I became the center of your attention.

III

With humans, all communication is very complex. On the one hand, there may be contradictions in the elements of the message. On the other hand, there may be confusion in the interpretation. A young lady is very flattering when calling one of her friends. Her friend wonders, "what does she want? Surely she will ask for something. How odd that she suddenly likes me so much!" Because some people have suffered many disappointments, betrayals and deceptions in their lives, they become suspicious and, with a very small amount of data, they interpret reality in the worst possible way. They do not build their interpretation based on their perceptions of body language, but on what they have learnt from previous experiences. Words are useless.

IV

A young man jumps into his girlfriend as she is in the middle of a very enthusiastic telephone call. He assumes that she is talking with another suitor and he sets up a scene of jealousy. She replies angrily, "what is wrong with you? I was congratulating my mom because she got an excellent deal on a house sale. What were you thinking? Are you crazy?" The boy's reaction to such a statement depends not on the girl's body language, but on his own emotional needs. What is it more important for him, to feel loved or does he prefer to feel hurt? At that precise moment, what does he need, a safety valve to relieve the guilt he feels for having abused his former girlfriend? Does he need to feel gloomy and sad? Does he want to be relaxed? Does he need comfort and protection? Does he need to let his anger out and express wrath? Does he require to justify his jealousy? Depending on what he emotionally needs, he will believe or not what his girlfriend tells him. The actual len-signs exchanged are not important. What matters is to fulfill the emotional needs of the moment.

V

We humans have lost the ability to interpret the messages we receive, we pay attention only to the meaning of words or react to them according to our emotional needs of the moment. This happens because we do not live in a group with only three to twenty individuals with whom we spend all our time. Human beings have to interact with hundreds of different people each week: cashiers, waiters, employees, customers, receptionists, subordinates, bosses, suppliers, coworkers, friends, acquaintances, classmates, in-laws, relatives and friends. Even with our closest group, we do not have much time to share. The words offer us an efficient means to communicate our intentions. In a few seconds you can tell a waiter that you want a cappuccino maple flavored, decaffeinated, with skim milk and sugar substitute. The message is clear and you expect to get what you ask for. You do not care if the waiter's body language indicates that he has a toothache.

VI

When a husband arrives home at night, his wife is sitting at the dining table, trying to make ends meet. She informs him that they have to pay the children's tuition, the mortgage of their department, the telephone and internet bills, their car allowance, and the balance of the credit card. The total amount they need is $6,000. After receiving this news, she gets up, goes to the kitchen, opens the refrigerator door, takes out a plate of beef stew and places it in the microwave for her husband to dine. She does not even notice the look of anguish on her husband's face because sales in his business have been very low. He has to pay $10,000 of wages and he does not know what to do. The husband has been so concerned about the situation of his business that he has not realized that it has been more than two weeks since the last time he was intimate with his wife. He is not able to perceive the signs of her increasing frustration and anger.

VII

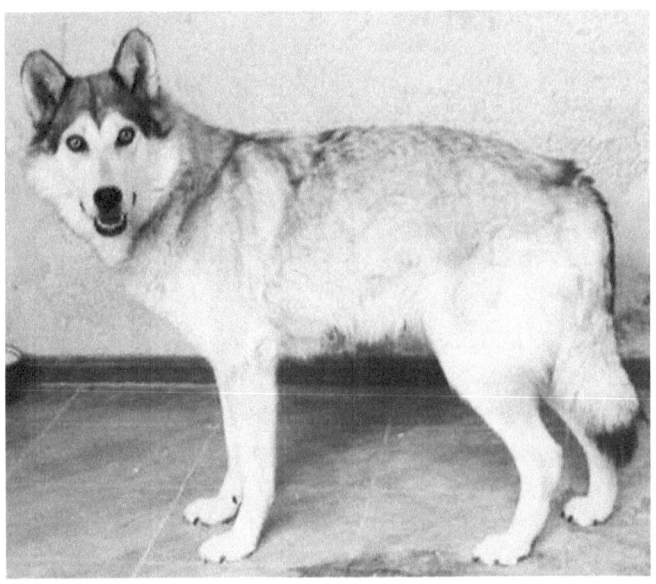

The language of a wolf pack is a highly sophisticated system that establishes, promotes, preserves or changes the emotional environment of the group.

The deep emotional bonding of the howling chorus, the thrill of the hunt, the anger of facing a threat, fear, joy, desire, love, every emotion is communicated through the language system.

A cub wolf tells his mother, "Mom, that old bitter female wolf said nnnuuuu to me." His mom asks him, "when she said that, did she have her ears forward or backward, a bristling mane? Was her tail up, horizontal, down or between her legs? What were you doing when the old wolf said nnnuuuu to you?" In other words, depending on the body language and the social context, nnnuuuu can have different meanings. This is a conclusion that applies to husband and wife communication, conversations between friends or the arguments between a boyfriend and his girlfriend. Words are not enough, context is everything.

CHAPTER 8

My love is a partially digested penguin

I

African wild dogs hunt in packs. After a successful hunt, they gorge on large chunks of meat and run back to the den where a litter of hungry cubs are waiting for them. The hunters regurgitate the food they have just eaten. Their stomachs have the same function as the pouch of a pelican that carries fish to her chicks. Bringing food to the cubs in their stomachs diminishes the risk of facing predators that might steal it.

II

National Geographic photographer Paul Nicklen went to Antarctica to film giant leopard seals. These seals measure up to 4 meters long, weigh 600 kg and feed mainly on penguins. Mr. Nicklen feared that these seals, eight times heavier than him, would attack him, but they did not.

A huge female seal began offering penguins to him. First, she gave him living penguins, but as the photographer let the penguins escape, the seal began to take weak and sick penguins to him. Of course, the photographer did not eat them. Then, the seal gave him dead penguins and finally she regurgitated partially digested penguins. The seal was offering her own food to the photographer. For a leopard seal, penguins are the most valuable thing they can offer. Penguins are its food, the fruit of its effort hunting.

III

In everyday life we are like leopard seals offering penguins to other people. Sometimes we fall madly in love and give everything we have to our beloved one.

The other person receives our love expressions and what he sees is a vomited penguin.

IV

There was a lady on TV talking about the hard chilaquiles she prepared. She explained the whole recipe. They were made of tortilla chips, complicated to fix. Tortillas must inflate when they are fried. The chips should be cut into perfect triangles and fried properly. When the chilaquiles were ready, they are used to build a structure of semitransparent corn, as fragile as a crystal. The sauce was poured just before eating, otherwise the chilaquiles would turn soft. The chicken meat should be cut in the smallest pieces, as fine as a white powder, larger chunks would make the structure collapse. Onion must also be chopped in small cubes. After six hours of preparation, hard chilaquiles were finally ready. When I went to the restaurant to eat them, I could not even try them because they were too spicy. For one person a plate is a sculpture of the Catalan Modernism in the style of Gaudí, made of corn, chicken breast, onion, salsa, sour cream and cheese. For another person it is a completely inedible dish.

V

My godmother was a leopard seal par excellence. Her dearest illusions were to prepare food and to feed people. After decades of studying, experimenting, learning recipes and discovering cooking secrets, she became an exceptional cook, extraordinary and acclaimed. That was, until the gradual loss of sight and her Parkinson made it impossible for her to cook. She could not approach her stew with her glasses to see if it had the right consistency, because the steam fogged her glasses. Due to the constant trembling of her hands, her skin burns were becoming more serious every day. When she realized that she could no longer cook, her life lost all meaning. What use was it for her to watch TV programs with recipes, if she would not be able to cook any more?

Finally my godmother came up with the perfect solution. She asked for filet mignon of exceptional quality, special potatoes, onion, imported Parmesan cheese and black pepper.

Once she had all the ingredients, she instructed Chucho, our manservant, to cut the meat into very thin slices. After explaining him how to carefully chop the onion, she told him how to put it to fry over very low heat in a little oil and when it had become a caramel, meat could be added. The meat had to be constantly turned so as not to burn. Then Chucho had to boil the potatoes, mash them and when they were at the perfect temperature, add the Parmesan cheese and pepper. If potatoes were too hot, cheese would melt completely and the mashed potatoes would become a gummy mass.

When I came to eat, my godmother had already told Chucho to set the table elegantly with her best dishes and cutlery. I sat. In front of me there was a plate filled with a scorched oil broth in which pieces of charred meat and chewy balls of pepper and potato floated. My godmother had imagined that she was offering me a luxurious dish, I sat with a regurgitated penguin in front of me.

VI

There is a terrible misunderstanding inherent to human communication. We invented languages that are perfect to tell stories. However, those languages describe reality subjectively. African wild dogs regurgitate food for the cubs, the message is perfectly clear, and they share their food in a joyous celebration. We humans have a mental image of things that does not correspond to the images other people have. I am writing an idea, you will read something completely different. I am offering you the best intellectual food I can cook, you will perceive a partially digested penguin. The magic of words is that anything can be misinterpreted in the worst possible ways.

CHAPTER 9

What Kind of Person Does This Make You?

I

Scientists who cling to the notion that animals possess a word language (a len-sign language in Pasolini's terms) fear that two dangers will become real if everybody accepts that animals do not talk. The first danger is to conclude that animals are not intelligent because they do not have a len-sign language. A lot of dog breeds, including Border Collies, and other animals as elephants, dolphins, killer whales, parrots, apes and many others have proven beyond any doubt that they have excellent memory and they are able to learn complex tasks, to solve problems, and to understand some of our len-signs. All these skills are clearly evidence of intelligence.

The second and graver danger is to conclude that if animals do not have a len-sign language, then they do not have an emotional life. This conclusion is absurd. There is no logic connection between the hypothesis and the conclusion. Yet, spokespeople from the cosmetic, pharmaceutical, and medical industries, who experiment with animals, conclude that the animals used in their experiments are not subject to deep physical and emotional suffering.

II

Emotions lie in a muddy region, nobody can really claim to be able to measure them. Many women, whose husbands are having an affair and are planning to divorce them, do not have a clue of what is happening and strongly believe that their men love them. People's feelings are fathomless, even with our highly specialized human len-sign languages and high standards of scientific criteria.

People lie about their feelings all the time. Some of you probably share not only a human len-sign language with your spouse, but also your house, your budget, and your vacations, and yet, how can you scientifically prove that he or she loves you? Many people claim that they do not know what they feel.

To prove the existence of love and other feelings is as impossible in human beings as it is in elephants, dogs, parrots or whatever intelligent creature you might suspect is capable of caring for another. You might remember a moment in your life when you were very sad, and yet you would not have any scientific tools to prove that fact.

If we believe that there is evidence that humans have feelings, the same evidence holds for some animals too, inconclusive in all cases. If animals have feelings, what right do we have to hurt them?

III

Human rights are not granted to people because they are intelligent. Due to accidents or disease, many people lose their cognitive abilities and memory and these unfortunate circumstances do not deprive them from their human rights. Human rights do not have anything to do with len-sign languages either. Newborn babies have not acquired a len-sign language and they hold their full rights. Human rights have the purpose of avoiding emotional, psychological and physical suffering. I cannot prove that you have feelings at all, but I expect you to have the right to live without the threat of suffering imposed on you by other human beings.

One thing is proven when someone concludes that, because animals do not have a len-sign language, then it is morally correct to deny them the right to live without inflicting them deliberate suffering. What is proven is that the person who reaches such a conclusion is not showing any logical intelligence. It would be as absurd as concluding that because your Alzheimer suffering grandmother does not have a len-sign language, then she should be deprived of her human rights.

In conclusion, animals might not have a len-sign language, but that does not mean that they are not intelligent or that they are not capable of deep feelings and emotions. Not having a len-sign language does not justify abusing them.

IV

There are two promising directions to try to understand the nonhuman mind. One direction would be to conduct nonintrusive, nonaggressive studies to understand the neurochemical reactions of dreaming and daydreaming of human beings and look for similar functions in other animal brains. The second way would be to study teaching, not learning in nonhuman animals. Dreaming and daydreaming give important clues to the content of thoughts. Teaching gives an insight of motivation and purpose.

V

With all these examples I have tried to show that len-sign languages are a very complex but incomplete part of our human relationships. If we want to understand the communication systems of other species, we would need to have a very clear idea of what we are looking for. Are we pretending to find in nonhuman animals a narrative driven, teaching language which is used to deceive and that promotes the neglect of other communication clues? Have we considered the possibility that animals might not have len-sign languages and might share im-signs (or echo-sign) languages, in which body language is a part of the image input? We need to carefully ponder what our human languages are and why such language characteristics would make sense in other environments in order to solve life problems different from the humans'.

www.ingramcontent.com/pod-product-compliance
Lightning Source LLC
Chambersburg PA
CBHW030524290526
45786CB00004B/1604